Con artist

Paul Conrad
30 YEARS WITH THE LOS ANGELES TIMES

Text by Norman Corwin
Introduction by Shelby Coffey III

Los Angeles Times, A Times Mirror Company, Los Angeles, California

Dedicated to the electorate who made this book possible—
and to the politicians who made it necessary.

Los Angeles Times

Publisher: David Laventhol
Editor: Shelby Coffey III

Project Director: Angela Rinaldi
Design/Production/Printing: Graphics Management, Inc.
Production Supervision: Bill Dorich
Art Director: Patricia Moritz
Cartoon Editor: Janet Nippell
Archival Research: Craig St. Clair

Library of Congress Catalogue Number: 93-78025

ISBN 0-9619095-5-2

A Times Mirror Company

Printed and bound in Singapore

Contents

It's not easy being a genius. Whether loved or hated, agreed with or scoffed at, whether subject of glowing awards or winning an honored spot on the White House "enemies list," it's broadly agreed that Paul Conrad is, in his field of editorial cartooning, a genius. In fact, the very name Conrad has for years provoked that broad gamut of emotions that certain single-name celebrities also produce like, say, Madonna. You wonder what in the world they've done now, or what they haven't done now.

Being a genius means winning the respect of your peers. As a three-time Pulitzer prize winner, one of the few such creatures ever to have existed, Paul Conrad certainly has that.

Since Otis Chandler, publisher of the Los Angeles Times, first hired him in 1964, he has afflicted the comfortable and comforted the afflicted. As Art Buchwald said: "Conrad's name strikes fear in the evil hearts of men all over the world…wherever there is corruption, greed or hypocrisy, everyone says, 'This is a job for Conrad.'"

Paul has that brand of genius which is more like that of the Old Testament prophets. He specializes in hairshirts and jeremiads and harpoons to the heart. He paints in sharp black and white, goes to the vulnerable core of the matter. Every one of us probably has favorite Conrads. And we've all had moments when we've been outraged that a hero has been taken to task.

Like other geniuses with a touch of marketing in their soul, Paul has taken advantage of found materials. California provided them in abundance—Richard Nixon and Ronald Reagan. If you are a friend, and forward enough, Paul will show you the special filling he has in his teeth with Richard Nixon's face drilled onto it. If you are lucky, you will remember the different ways Ronald Reagan has

appeared in Conrad's cartoons. He has been everything from King Kong, to Professor Henry Higgins, Uncle Sam, King Henry VIII, a shogun warrior, a vulture, a scarecrow, a panhandler, a jailbird, a dunce, a clown, the warhead of a nuclear missile and God Almighty. While Paul never sent a cash donation to the Reagan Library, he did once hold the Nixon Chair at Whittier College.

As a mark of his genius, it hasn't always been easy for those who stood near him and supported him. David Halberstam writes about the phone calls Governor Reagan used to make in the morning to Otis Chandler to complain about the latest drawing. After a while, it's written, Otis quit taking the calls. But then Nancy started to call him to say Ron's breakfast had been ruined again. But those calls were so frequent, says Halberstam, Otis finally had to quit taking them, too.

As with a lot of geniuses, his allies are true partisans. During the Gulf crisis, Paul had a cartoon of Saddam Hussein showing his hindquarters to the world captioned with something like the phrase, "Moon over Baghdad." Tony Day and Tom Plate, editors of the editorial pages, have always worked artfully with Paul in the great give-and-take that goes on between editors and great editorial cartoonists; but this time the cartoon was bumped up to my office. I kept suggesting alternatives to Saddam's hindquarters, and eventually that particular cartoon didn't run; but it circulated like literature of the repressed Russian samizdat. It found its way into the wayward press as an example of shocking censorship—though it was never exactly censored, we just ran out of alternatives to Hussein's big bottom.

I was rewarded for that effort with a nice letter saying, as memory serves, "Dear Sir: You dumb son-of-a-bitch. Your job is to hire talented people like Paul Conrad, give them free rein and get out of their way." Which is an excellent job description for an editor—up to a point.

Not that Paul needs that much protection, because he is the kind of genius who gives as good as he gets. He has a sign on his desk that says "You voted for him." And though he was sued unsuccessfully for libel for portraying an oil executive as Scrooge during the '70's oil crisis, that same executive asked for an original Conrad years later when Paul took his side of an argument.

The only thing that gives as much pleasure as defending Paul, actually, is provoking him. He especially enjoys it if you walk by his office in the afternoon while he's watching the hearings on the latest scandal from Washington or Sacramento on CNN and say to him, "Gee, I wish I had a nice job watching TV and then drawing little pictures about it that make so many people so angry that the Circulation Department will be answering calls till half-past ten tomorrow morning."

He loves giving looks that could kill. But then we voted for him. And we still do.

Shelby Coffey III
Editor and Executive Vice President
Los Angeles Times

the Sixties

Had there been a Paul Conrad and a free press to print him in the Athens of Pericles, or in the time of the Caesars, those eras would be illuminated by a sort of polarized light, and we would enjoy a fuller knowledge of the ancient world than we owe to the diligence of Plutarch and Gibbon. Scholars and historians across centuries would have consulted every last cartoon, and certainly surviving prints would be preserved today as treasures in the great museums.

If this premise is granted, which is not hard to do, there can be little doubt that the work of the living Conrad, together with that of his sharpest contemporaries, will in the future be sought and closely studied. For even though today's infinitely expanding archives bulge with records of just about everything held to be significant, we find ourselves oftener than not turning to the charged vision, the gut response, the slant, even the bias, of the political cartoonist, to get a visceral interpretation of what goes on around us. A master of the art like Conrad abstracts and epitomizes so effectively that, like radar, he penetrates smoke and mist.

"Caricatures," said Emerson, "are often the truest history of the times." We do not have to agree with the caricaturist to agree with Emerson, for whether we like a cartoon or not, we recognize it for its force, for the point it makes.

In the following pages are distilled four decades of turbulent events—wars, riots, massacres, assassinations, the ongoing struggle for civil rights, poverty, homelessness, corruption, national scandals, malfeasance, crime, snarling confrontations over abortion and environment, stresses and upheavals in foreign and domestic policy. Yet Conrad's view of these is almost unfailingly provocative. By turns he is stark, bitter, angry, grieving, joyous, subtle, contemptuous, scathing. And also funny. At least four cartoons in this group culled from the Sixties are entertaining, whether one goes along with them or not. They depict Barry Goldwater as Goldilocks, Everett Dirksen and Lyndon Johnson as the Walrus and Carpenter of *Alice in Wonderland* and Ronald Reagan as a one-man band. Practically all of Conrad's drawings, whether funny or grave, have power; they all are weapons in an extraordinary arsenal, and he does not hesitate to use them.

In the accounting of Conrad, the Sixties were dominated by the war in Vietnam, chronic U.S.- Soviet antagonism and early pages in the Iliad of the civil rights movement. Among principal figures making brief appearances are the Kennedy brothers John and Ted, Khrushchev, Reagan, Martin Luther King, Jr. and Hubert H. Humphrey.

"Stand back everybody! He's got a bomb!!"

NEW ALABAMA RIOT
Police Dogs, Fire Hoses Ha[...]

"Fifteen yards for pushing!"   "Fifteen yards for holding!"

'Anybody got a match?'

'…the Great Buddha has answered our prayers!'

"It looked back!"

"Well, if their money is good enough for the Canadians, it's good enough for me!"

'All those in favor of the test-ban treaty will signify…'

"The time has come," the Walrus said, "to talk of many things: Of cloture votes, and civil rights, and Martin Luther Kings."

"Shall we be trotting home again?" But answer came there none—
And this was scarcely odd, because they'd eaten every one.

'Someone's been eating my porridge,' said the Daddy Bear.

Only the names have been changed.

'10...9...8...7...6...5...'

"I call on every law enforcement officer…"
–President Johnson

A Letter from the Front

"Take me to a leader!"

"You've mentioned unemployment, housing, education, police brutality, and despair…but, what was the reason for the riot?"

"There's a lady out in Mason City, Iowa,
he can't seem to convince!"

"First, Premier Ky, you must learn the principles of democracy..."

"Tenting tonight, Tenting tonight, Tenting on the Old School Ground."

"Excuse me…I thought that sort of thing was unconstitutional!"

Majority Whip

"Wha'd'ya mean…'He doesn't know the territory'…?"

"You've seen one redwood,
you've seen 'em all!"

—Ronald Reagan

Flag Razing in Central Park

"Pick a number between 20,000 and 100,000…"

"Martin Luther who…?"

Speaking of forcing North Vietnam
to its knees…

"Don't turn my dream into a nightmare…!"

Reflecting Pool

MPHIS

ONE AND ONE-HALF
MILLION
PRIMARY VOTES
FOR KENNEDY

"It became necessary to destroy the party to save it!"

"…Fascist…!"

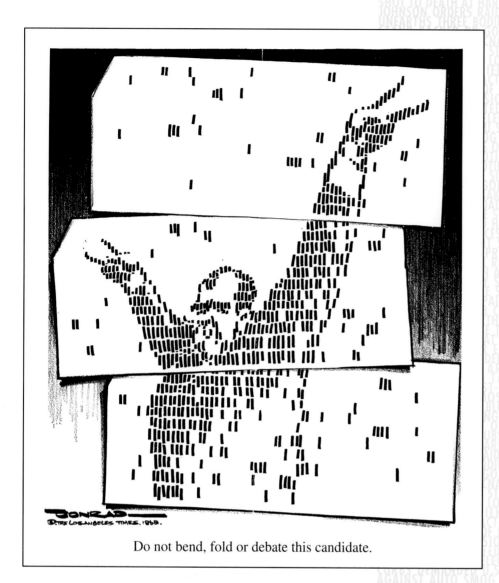

Do not bend, fold or debate this candidate.

"I've got to go now…
I've been appointed Secretary of Defense
and the Secret Service men are here!"

MPHREY

'Ye shall find the babe wrapped in swaddling clothes, lying in a manger.'

Manrise

WALK ON MOON

'That's One Small Step for Man...
One Giant Leap for Mankind'

"If you don't mind, Senator Kennedy, I'd rather walk…"

The Sound of Marching Effete

the Seventies

Historians of the written word are expected to be tidy, if not fastidious; to weigh, sift and explicate, to support texts with footnotes, appendices, bibliographies and other scaffoldings of research. Not so the editorial cartoonist. He renders history after his own fashion, and, if he is masterful at it, his version can be more persuasive than exegetical script.

Conrad is masterful at it. Never mind his three Pulitzer prizes. His genius has been acknowledged day in and day out by the delight, or pain, with which his work is received, depending of course on the bearing of the viewer. And there is always plenty to bear.

The cartoons of the Seventies reflect a broadening of the concerns of the Sixties. The war in Vietnam becomes increasingly unpopular, thanks in part to such ghastly side effects as the massacre at My Lai and the murder of demonstrating students in Ohio and Mississippi. Watergate develops into a malignancy so virulent that a President has to be cut out. Twice in a series of Watergate cartoons, Shakespeare is called on to deal with Richard Nixon, first with a quote from *Richard II,* then as Hamlet soliloquizing over the skulls of multiple Yoricks.

Conrad's imagination ranges with equal agility over foreign and domestic subjects. The vexations of Israel and her enemies are registered, and for a spell there is hope for conciliation in the interlude, all too brief, that starts with Menachem Begin welcoming Anwar Sadat at the inn, and moves on to Jimmy Carter straining to push both uphill at Camp David.

Chile, Panama and world hunger share space in the decade along with the Shah of Iran and his successor, the Ayatollah Khomeini. There are reflections on domestic poverty, education, pollution, the gun lobby, abortion, the death penalty, the Equal Rights Amendment, Jerry Brown, greedy oil companies ("Oilatollahs"), California Supreme Court Justice Rose Bird as martyr, Jimmy Carter's lust-in-my-heart confession, the plight of farm workers in California, commercial trash on TV, Gerald Ford pardoning himself for pardoning Nixon, and a bulldog-faced J. Edgar Hoover being watched approvingly by cigar-smoking mafia cats as he chases Black Panthers—a presage of allegations to be made 25 years later involving Hoover's suzerainty over the FBI. Also in this slim folio, one of Conrad's wryest cartoons, in which Hoover is assigned to the back seat of a bus driven by Martin Luther King, Jr.

LIEUTENANT CHARGED WITH MUR

Poll reports more Americans disturbed over My Lai publicity
than My Lai massacre itself.

"Shut it down! Shut it down! Shut it down!"

"Son…!"   "Dad…!"

Blanket Party

"HIT 'EM AGAIN—HIT 'EM AGAIN—
HARDER—HARDER!"

"F.B.Me…Hoover speaking…"

There are cats and there are fat cats…

PRISON STORMED
9 Hostages, 28 Convicts Killed

"Oh, it's just kind of a hobby with me…!"

"It only hurts when I laugh!"

Reagan Hood — He Takes From the Poor and Gives to the Rich!

"…one nation, divisible, with liberty and justice for some."

The Light at the End of the Tunnel

"…Four more years? Four more years?…"

"Let's overthrow the government!" "Which government?"

MILITARY SEIZES POWER IN CHILE
Allende Reportedly Kills Self

"He says he's from the phone company…"

You know nothing about Watergate. Which group would you most likely suspect of burglary, theft, breaking and entering, wiretapping, election law violations, and conspiracy?

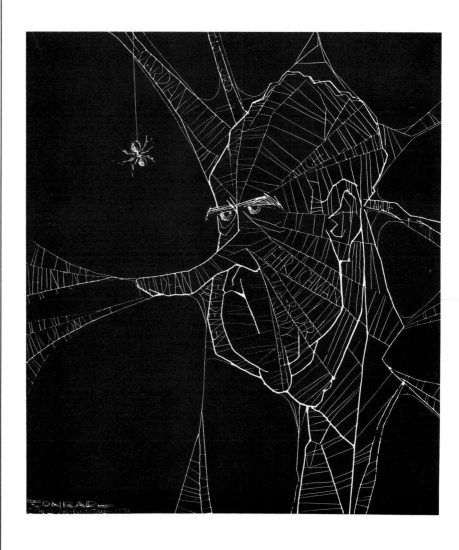

His Own Worst Enemy

"YOU'RE sick of hearing about Watergate!"

"Oh, nothing much…what's new with you, John?"

O that I were as great as my grief, or lesser than my name!
Or that I could forget what I have been!
Or not remember what I must be now!

King Richard II—Act III, Scene III.

"Alas, poor Agnew, Mitchell, Stans, Ehrlichman, Haldeman, Dean, Kalmbach, LaRue, Mardian, Strachan, McCord, Liddy, Chapin, Hunt, Colson, Krogh, Magruder, Young—I knew them…"

The King is Dead—
Long Live the Presidency!

Turning the Economy Around

"I pledge allegiance to the flag of the country that gives me the best deal…"

"And the first shall be last and the last first."

'Victory finds a hundred fathers—defeat is an orphan.'

HO CHI MINH

'Our long national nightmare is over…'

"I was maybe the last Vietnam casualty."

Stoop Labor

"My name is Juan Garcia and I could use your help here in California!"

"Brother Brown is in conference…
can I help you?"

"It looks like Brother Brown has gone over the wall!"

"…1980 on your dial…"

"No country has ever observed the terms of a treaty if it suited its national purposes to break that treaty." –Reagan on the Panama Canal Treaty

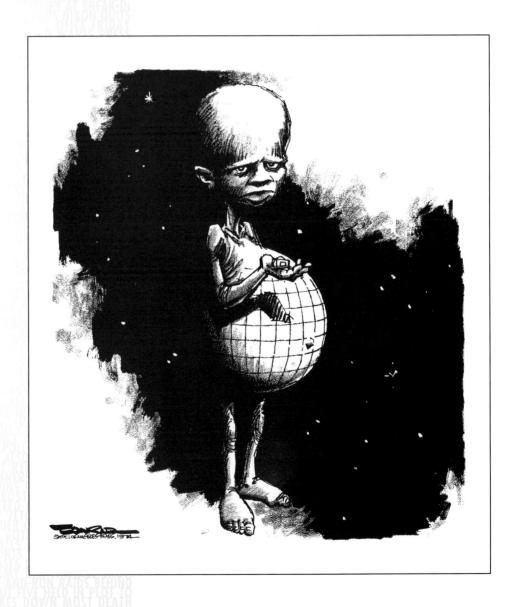

'Forgive them, Father, for they know not what they do…'

The Butcher's Thumb

61

"There's no waste problem...
we just dig a new new hole!"

"You wanta take away our gusto…?"

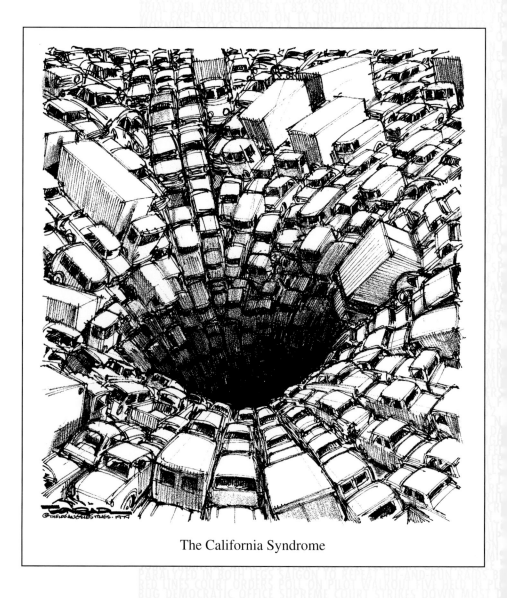

The California Syndrome

Hara-Cari

Vatican prohibits ordination of women as priests because Christ's representatives must have a 'natural resemblance' to him.

"Joan, you still have time to recant!"

"Sexism, hell! We did the same thing to Earl Warren!"

BAKKE WINS BUT JUSTICES UPHOLD
AFFIRMATIVE ACTION

Black Teen-agers 40% Unemployed

Speaking of child pornography…

...and for those who made the 1977 Nobel
Peace Prize necessary...

Latter-Day Israelites Wandering 40 Years
in the Wilderness

A future Horowitz, a future Einstein,
a future Salk…

The Eighth Wonder of the World

The Oilatollah Khompanies

"…Decontrol!…Decontrol!…Decontrol!…"

"Do I hear $225,000…?"

"Now that the issues have become more manageable…"

"Entrapment!"

Lord of the Flies

"You people are nothing but functional illiterates anyway!"

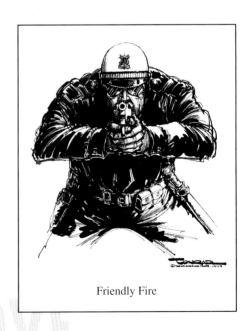

Friendly Fire

the Eighties

Paul Conrad found in Ronald Reagan a long-running and fertile subject. With tenacity as well as virtuosity, he tracked the ex-actor's career from his candidacy for the governorship of California, through twelve years of state and federal administration, to his post-presidency trip to Japan, a visit that paid two million dollars and upon which Conrad does not neglect to comment.

There was very little middle ground anywhere on Reagan. Ardent supporters ranked him as one of the great presidents, opponents abominated him as one of the worst. Conrad inclined to the second group, depicting Reagan in his cartoons as venal, black-hearted, ungifted, a reactionary, a hawk, a blockhead, a dissembler, a union-buster, a buck-passer, a toady to the rich and scorner of the poor, an amiable mediocrity with a penchant for disastrous appointments, persistently misspoken, a dodger deeply rehearsed in shifting blame when things went wrong.

Of more than a hundred cartoons in this segment from the eighties, almost a third relate to Reagan and present him in many guises—as a robot, a puppeteer, a tattooed man, a clown, a gangster, a face on a barroom floor, Reagan Hood ("robs the poor to pay the rich"), a hawk giving himself a fix with a bayonet, an escape artist, a clone of Moammar Kadafi, a Napoleonic figure, as an ex-president up for sale. Some of the settings in which we find him are just as bizarre—in a bathtub, in a urinal, in a slum, in the Vatican.

Democrats of rank do not fare much better, particularly Mondale, Hart, Carter and Brown, but then for most of the four decades represented in this volume, Democrats were not in office, hence were not the most conspicuous targets. Conrad's raw meat consisted mainly of highly placed Republicans, including one related by marriage. Nancy Reagan comes in for selected ribbing, especially in a famous cartoon titled *The Sorcerer's Apprentice,* alluding to her engagement of an astrologer for guidance in the timing of certain presidential activities.

As usual with Conrad the world is brought into his drawings: Poland, Argentina, El Salvador, Nicaragua, the Soviet Union, Iran, the Middle East, Perestroika, the breaching of the Wall. (Incidentally, if ever there was a model of furious action in a cartoon, it is the depiction of two soccer players, Begin of Israel and the PLO, going after a ball that is the globe we live on.)

Conrad does not let down on events and issues. Poverty, urban riots, the deficit, the Reagan court, the economy, the cost of Pentagon nuts and bolts, ludicrous nuclear defense proposals, Oliver North, leveraged buyouts, AIDS, failures of deregulation, the greenhouse effect, a structure of symbolic pendants titled *Popemobile,* the demise of the CIA's William J. Casey, drawn resting in his coffin ("You *can* take it with you!") at a time when he was ripe for investigation of complicity in the Iran-Contra shambles.

Also in this decade Conrad demonstrates that he can change his mind. He vigorously reverses his position on abortion as expressed earlier by the drawing of a crucified infant. In the boldest of three cartoons, the reproductive area of a nude woman is covered with a notice reading, "State Gov't Property / U.S. Supreme Court."

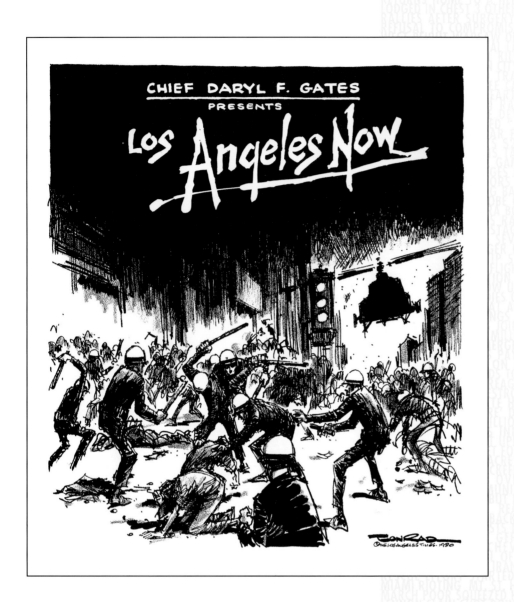

"I pick my arrows out of thin air.'"

"You look for a certain compatibility, a broad compatibility, with your own philosophy in looking for judges." –Reagan

"You don't look truly needy to me...
Needy, perhaps, but not truly needy!"

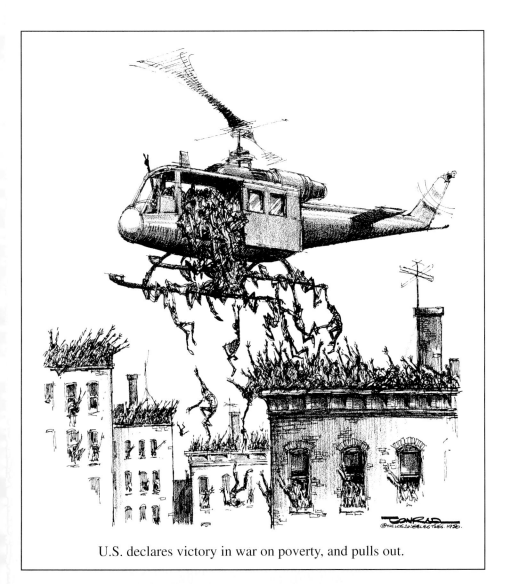

U.S. declares victory in war on poverty, and pulls out.

"What's so terrible about 'black lung'…?"

LIVING PROOF THAT GUNS DON'T NECESSARILY KILL PEOPLE…!

NATIONAL RIFLE ASSOCIATION
WASHINGTON, D.C.

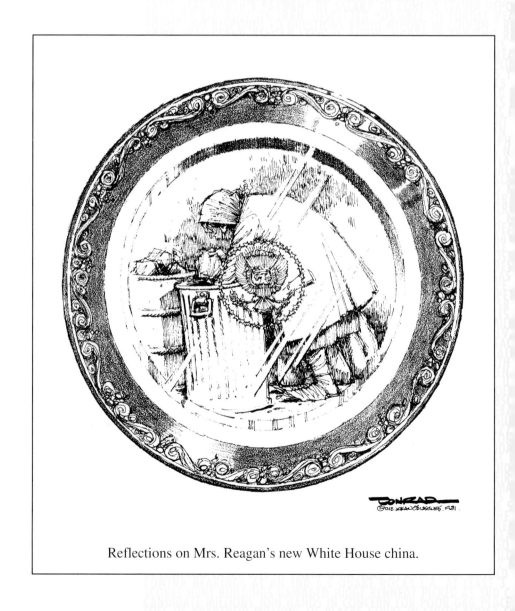

Reflections on Mrs. Reagan's new White House china.

Trickle-down theory.

The first notch.

DEAR GOV. DEUKMEJIAN:
WHO PAID FOR **YOUR**
EDUCATION?

"Gov. Deukmejian, you are charged with vetoing
the strip-and-search bill…Please bend over…"

Affixing blame for our economic problems.

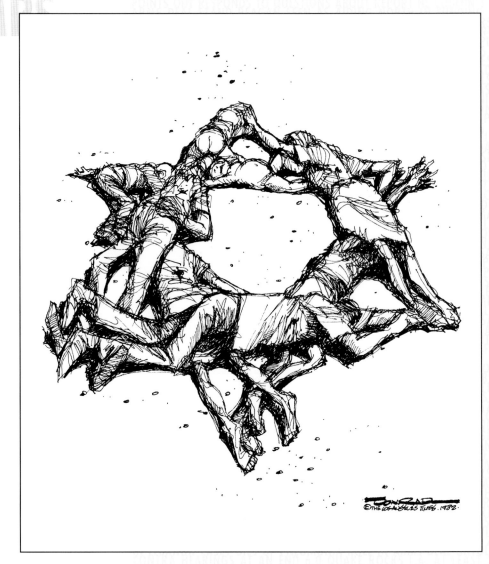

El Salvador

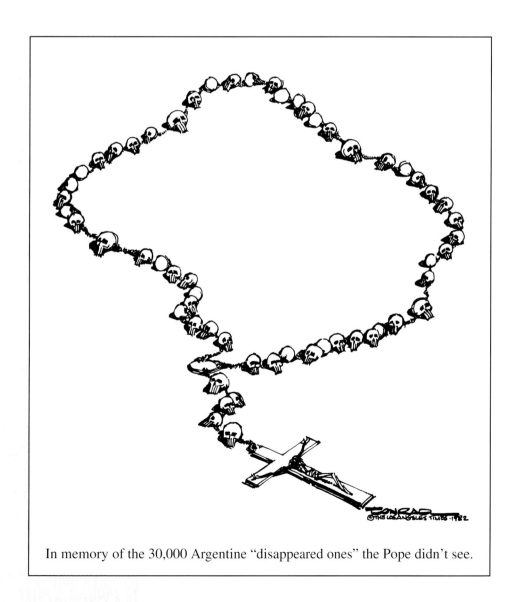

In memory of the 30,000 Argentine "disappeared ones" the Pope didn't see.

"Then it's agreed…You'll take care of the poor and I'll take care of the rich!"

"Well, tell him to turn up his hearing aid!"

The War Powers Actor

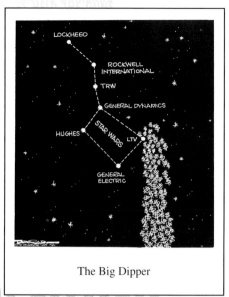

The Big Dipper

DEFENSE SPENDING

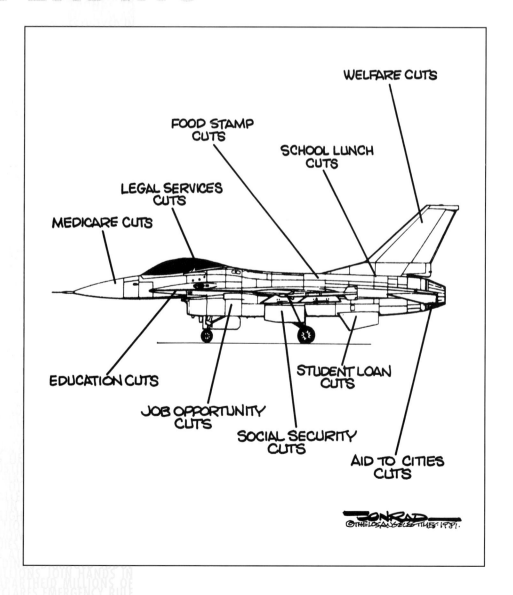

"We'll bury you!"

Administration's civil-defense plan for nuclear war.

"I'm willing to discuss the arms race whenever those Russian devils are!"

JUSTICES EASE CURBS ON
NUCLEAR WASTE DISPOSAL

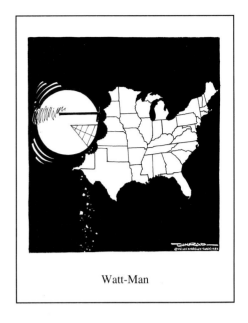

Watt-Man

"I'm nobody's puppet!"

103

"Now, about the rules…"

The Tell-Tale Hart

"WE ARE somebody…!"

"Let's face it, Fritz—You're no Harry
Truman, and I'm no Lauren Bacall!"

"Religion and politics are necessarily related." –Reagan

"You're on your own, kid, once you're born!"

FACTUAL ERRORS
IN SPEECHES
WASH RIGHT OUT

REPELS BLAME FOR
CENTRAL AMERICA
TERRORISM

HOLDS SHAPE
IN SPITE OF
MIDEAST
PEACE PLAN FIASCO

WON'T ABSORB
CRITICISM OF
ECONOMIC POLICIES
FAVORING RICH

WRINKLE-FREE DESPITE
DOMESTIC SPENDING CUTS

RESISTS BEIRUT
BLOOD STAINS

SHEDS LINT AND
$200 BILLION DEFICITS

DISPELS BLAME
FOR APPOINTEES
LIKE: WATT,
CASEY, BURFORD,
MEESE, ETC.

WON'T FADE DESPITE
MASSIVE DEFENSE SPENDING

The Man in the Teflon-Coated Suit

"My candle burns at both ends; It will not last the night;
But, ah, my foes, and, oh, my friends—It gives a lovely light."
–Edna St. Vincent Millay

Vast worldwide misinformation machine.

People want to believe.

"I've never worn makeup."

"Four more years!"

"Let's walk Gramm, Rudman and Hollings to get to Reagan!"

"Have I got a deal for you!"

The difference between 'overt' and 'covert' CIA military actions.

"Nicaraguan *contras*…the moral equal of our Founding Fathers." –Reagan

"Don't none of you sanctuary people move!"

U.S. BOMBS LIBYA

"We have done what we had to do.
If necessary, we will do it again."

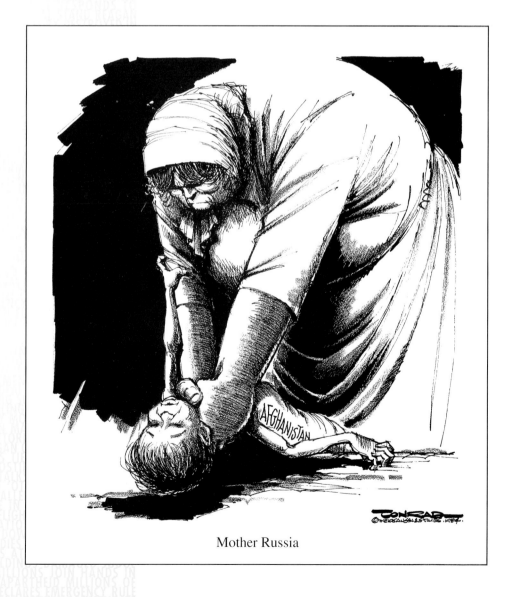

Mother Russia

Ask not for whom the reactor tolls; it tolls for thee.

Three-minute egg.

SHUTTLE EXPLODES; ALL 7 DIE

...and touched the face of God. –John Magee Jr.

O-ring

121

Photo opportunity.

The knock on the bedroom door.

"And I resent the left-wing attempts to
politicize my Supreme Court appointments!"

"Justice Rehnquist, will you be wearing your hooded white
or your black robe today?"

The poor don't know where to go to get food. –President Reagan

Home for Christmas

"It's a privilege to shake the hand of a freedom fighter!"

S.A. DECLARES EMERGENCY RULE

1,200 Rounded Up

Reagan Administration's moral compass.

The naked truth.

Ollie's World

THE EIGHTIES

"We needed a ship." –Col. North

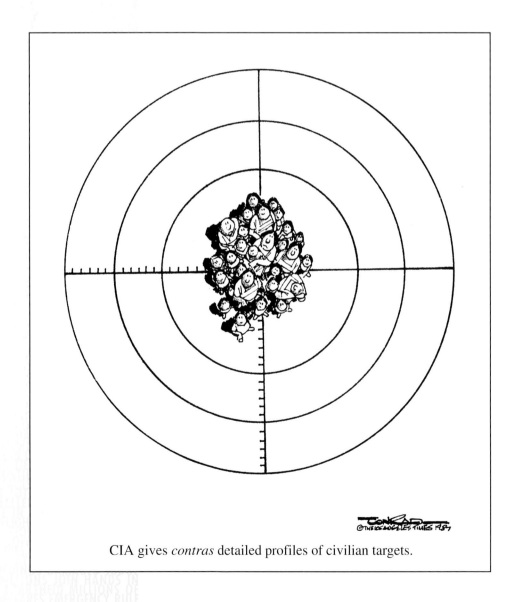

CIA gives *contras* detailed profiles of civilian targets.

"Thank you for not smoking."

CASEY DIES OF PNEUMONIA, ROLE IN ARMS DEAL UNTOLD

You *can* take it with you!

Conscience of a conservative.

"We don't do junk bonds anymore…
just bail bonds!"

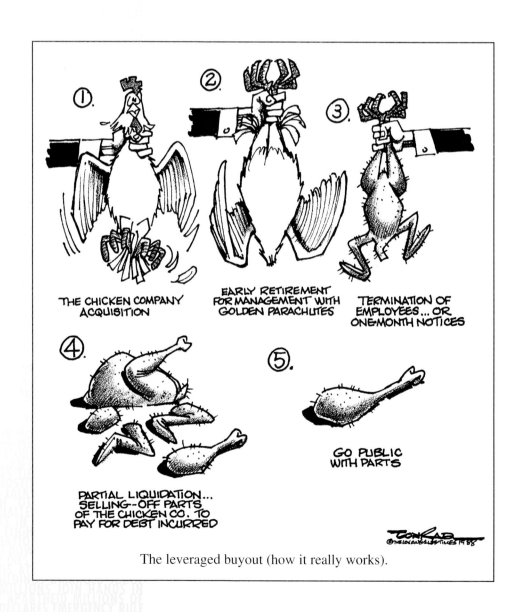

The leveraged buyout (how it really works).

The American Banking Association's
drive-thru window.

Hands Across America

"Can't you see that we're busy with this humanitarian liver transplant?"

The President faces the AIDS question.

Speaking of the need for condoms…

Administration war against drugs in Bolivia...and in the U.S.A.

The Sorcerer's Apprentice

Another gang terrorizing U.S. cities.

Morning in America

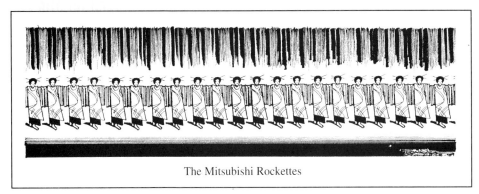

The Mitsubishi Rockettes

... and to our children and to their children and to their childrens' children. I leave the remainder of my estate, the debt of two and one-half trillion dollars....

Drawing up the will.

Abraham and Isaac

The greenhouse effect.

Nuclear weapons plant.

Acid rain.

Jesse Jackson's grandmother's quilt.

Popemobile

No Heart   No Brains   No Courage

Passing the torch.

"Horseshoes, Lee—just horseshoes!"

Dear Mr. President:
Too bad about William Lucas. However, if you are still looking for a black to serve as head of the Civil Rights Division — one who contributed greatly to your campaign and has Court experience, I would appreciate being considered. Sincerely,
Willie Horton

Monument to the First Amendment

"The Face on the Barroom Floor"

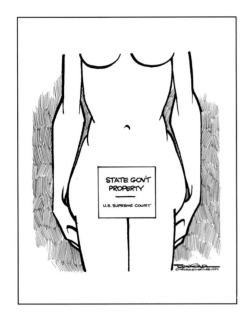

"Their daddy, George Deukmejian, doesn't believe in family planning."

UPHOLDS STATES' AUTHORITY BUT RETAINS
ROE VS. WADE

Molested by her father, raped by a stranger,
abandoned by her President.

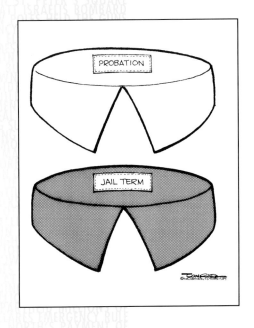

Prospective jurors for the North trial
who have no knowledge of the Iran-Contra affair.

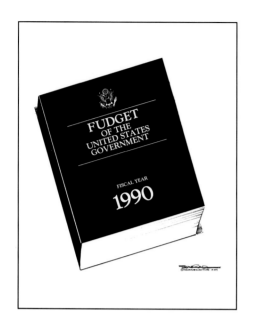

FOR A NEW POLITICAL CAREER

FOR THE POOR

FOR A LOWER HANDICAP

FOR SALE

The Ex-Presidents at Work

"It's Frankie…just say no."

El Salvador

El Salvador

Humpty Dumpty sat on a wall…

the Nineties

The strength and emotional voltages of Conrad's work proceed from tenets he has openly expressed. "Editorial cartoonists," he once wrote, "are idealists of another world. Political, social and moral injustices are perceived as monstrosities. Put intensity of conviction in the hands of a determined artist and you have the basic ingredients of a cartoonist—to care and to care deeply; to sweep aside all the complexities and go to the basic issue; to take suspicions, confidences and past events, and record them larger than life.

Conrad has sustained that credo, which in turn has sustained him. As this volume goes to press, the last decade of the century is a third gone, yet there is no slackening of force, no retreat, no weakening of conviction, no drying up the aquifer of humor. Like Nolan Ryan in middle age, Conrad still throws hard. He has never been interested in pleasing all of the people even part of the time, he regards the avoidance of controversy as a form of eunuchism, and he does not believe in the bland leading the bland.

Prime among subjects recruited to Conrad's gallery in the Nineties was, of course, George Bush, seen here in various contexts including foot-dragging on health care, the arming of Saddam Hussein pre-Kuwait, the blood, sand and oil of Desert Storm, accommodation of Arab despots, a soft spot for luxury yacht owners, the "family values" rhetoric, unanswered questions about Iraqgate, the pardoning of Caspar Weinberger, Elliott Abrams and others left over from the Iran-Contra hearings, the stumbling campaign for re-election, the ultimate defeat—the last of these mourned by Conrad in a self-portrait of mock distress, because he, cartoonist by appointment to a million readers daily, was losing a prime target.

New exhibits in Conrad's gallery of the Nineties are Dan Quayle, John Sununu, Supreme Court Justice Clarence Thomas (pygmytized in the chair of retired Thurgood Marshall), the Clintons, the Rodney King beating ("One picture is worth zero"), a riot-wracked Los Angeles.

And again the world is present: South Africa's Nelson Mandela ("One man, 28 million votes"); Gorbachev and his crumbling U.S.S.R; a forlorn Yeltsin; a bleeding Sarajevo; the hanging tree of the death squads of El Salvador.

Again, and as always, there are cartoons which carry metaphor to poetic heights—in this section alone, the F-117A hummingbird that consumes twice its body weight daily; the Little Rock vs. Big Rock; the body bag of gays killed by "friendly fire."

Voltaire, a liberal maverick who would have treasured Conrad, wrote that history can be well written only in a free country. The same may be said about drawn history. It is testimony to the vigor of a free press in America, and to the country itself, that an artist with the passions and convictions of Conrad can present one or another President as a public executioner, a gangster, a terrorist, a robber, an alligator, a frog, a dead fish, a bunny, a dog, a chimp, a hen, a cow, a troglodyte, a liar, a scoundrel, Jekyll and Hyde, Macbeth, Popeye, a nuclear warhead, a puppet, a submerged mine, a bullfighter, a pumpkinhead and a prostrate Gulliver without being hounded, picketed, sued, blacklisted, exiled or, as was the case with Daumier and his publisher, sent to prison.

It is also a tribute to the integrity of the Los Angeles Times that it has long been Conrad's home and window to his art through thick and thin, war and peace, boom and bust, medals and mud. Years ago an editor of the Times, Bill Thomas, wrote, "There is little doubt that genuine anguish has been felt by those whose convictions are deeply offended by (Conrad's) judgments...but it is necessary to explain at the same time that the message being conveyed usually is not essentially different from those expounded in newspaper opinion columns, and it would thus be illogical to forbid the cartoonist his message simply because the manner of conveyance is different....It's been a real trial on occasion to have been editor through 14 years of Conrad, but it's been a rare treat, too. For Conrad is the best there is."

He can say that again.

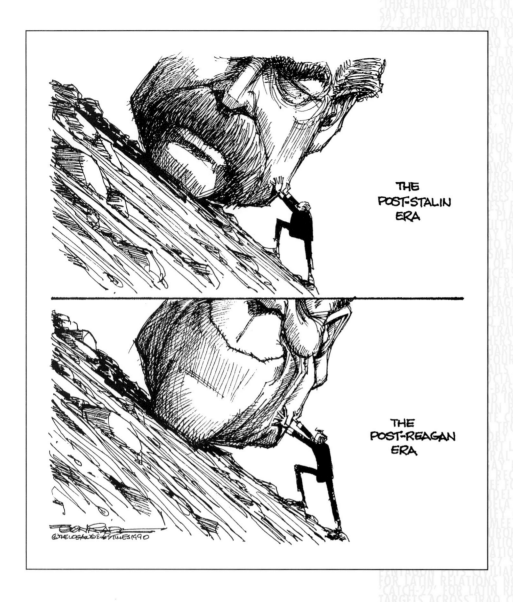

THE
POST-STALIN
ERA

THE
POST-REAGAN
ERA

GORBACHEV AND KOHL SWEEP AWAY
FINAL BARRIERS TO UNIFICATION

World War II ain't over
'til the fat lady sings!

One man, 28 million votes.

USS KINDER

USS GENTLER

The hummingbird consumes twice its own body weight daily.

If you thought Dukakis looked silly in that tank…

169

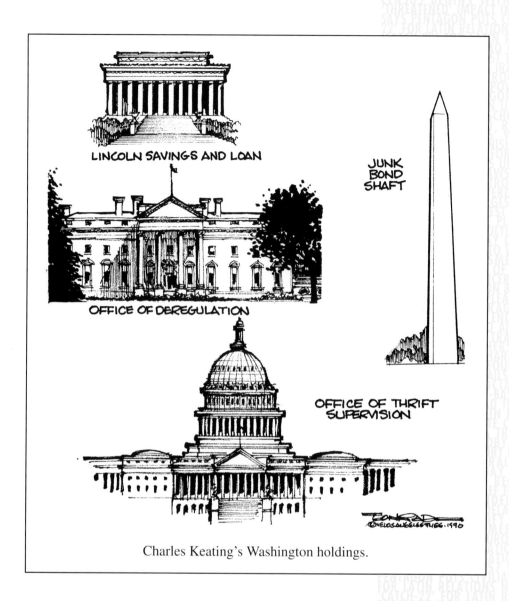

LINCOLN SAVINGS AND LOAN

OFFICE OF DEREGULATION

JUNK BOND SHAFT

OFFICE OF THRIFT SUPERVISION

Charles Keating's Washington holdings.

2 Live Crew

A jury to decide obscenity laws.

"Dad, they're calling up the reserves!"

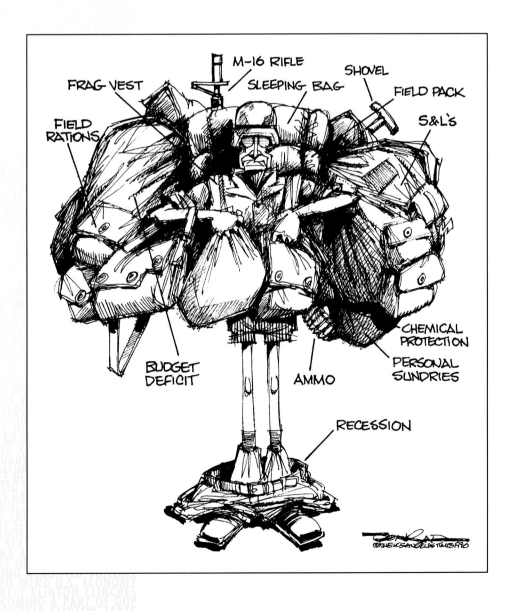

"Keep going! The line Bush drew
in the sand is here someplace!"

Reaganstein's Saddam

"Wolfe was right.
You can't go home again."

Bush's thousand points of light.

Saddam Hussein sat on a wall,
Saddam Hussein refuses to fall...

U.S. FORGING SANCTIONS PLAN TO OUS

HUSSEIN

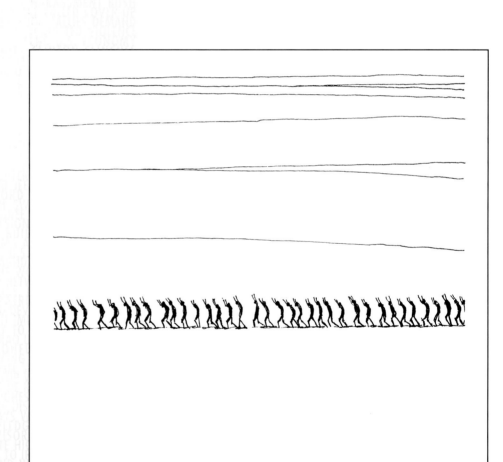

Line in the sand.

Joe Rosenthal's photo of the flag-raising on Iwo Jima if journalists had been pooled in World War II.

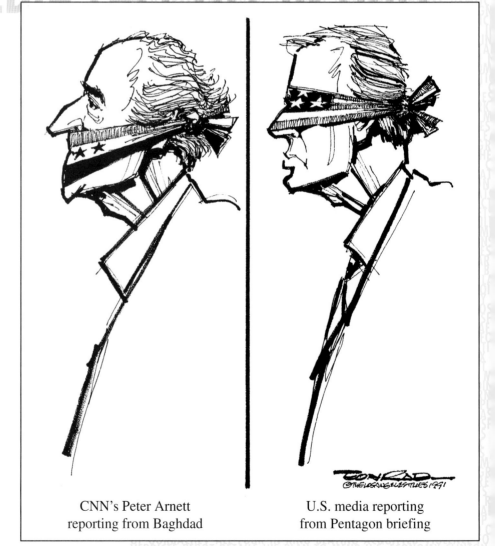

CNN's Peter Arnett reporting from Baghdad

U.S. media reporting from Pentagon briefing

The Republican Guard

"I have drawn a line in the blood."

The homecoming parade.

Dances with Wolves

FRAGILE EMPIRE CRUMBLING EAS

Mother Russia

THE EDUCATION PRESIDENT

THE ENVIRONMENTAL PRESIDENT

THE CIVIL RIGHTS PRESIDENT

THE TRANSPORTATION PRESIDENT

"We come to bury Cranston,
not to praise him…"

Death Row

Justice Thurgood Marshall sat here.

"Seen any good porno movies lately?"

WOULD YOU BUY A **USED** CAR FROM THIS MAN?

WOULD YOU BUY A **NEW** CAR FROM THIS MAN?

BUSH VOWS FIGHT ON HARD TIMES

He Calls for Tax Changes

Bush seeks to kill luxury tax on yachts.

"Well, there goes the neighborhood!"

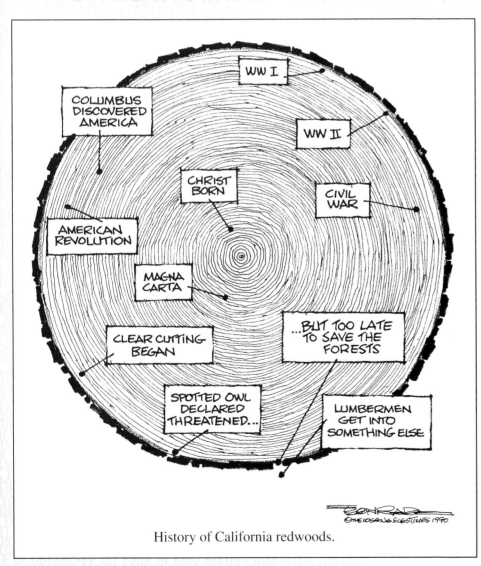

History of California redwoods.

The Melted Pot

One picture is worth zero

189

YOU BUILD A PARTY, THEY'LL COME!

The Final Four

When the going gets tough, the tough get going.

Family Values

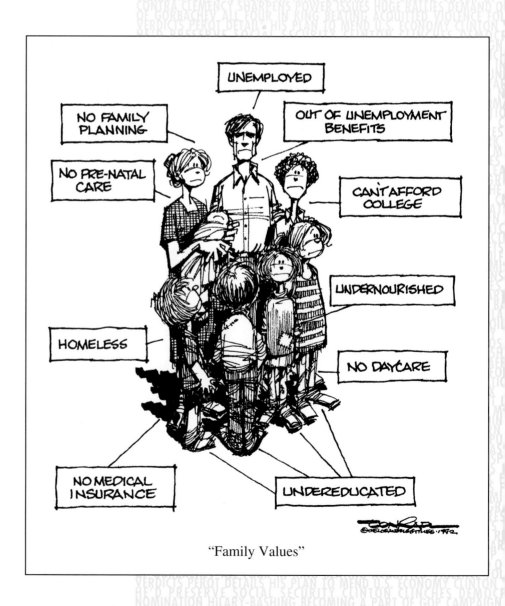

"Family Values"

"What do you wanta' be if you grow up?"

"We have a totally clear conscience." –Bush Administration

What to do about Iraqgate.

...And now for the *real* trick!

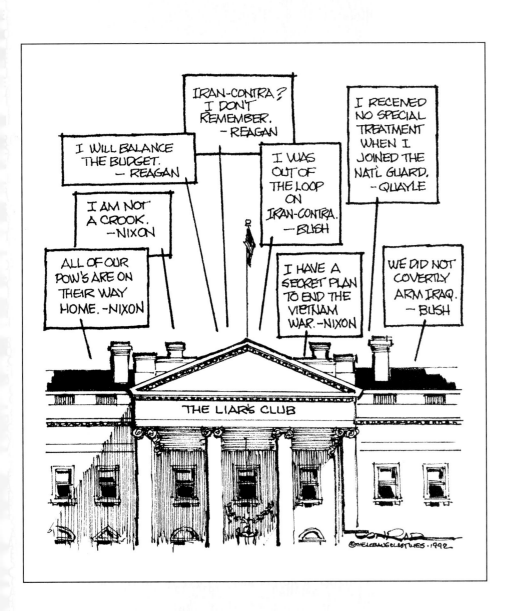

The Reagan Bush

Pardons happen.

The Nine Lives of Richard Nixon

Pillory Clinton

"Shoot, if you must, this old gray head,
but spare your country's flag," she said.
                    -Barbara Frietchie Bush

Dish Raising at Mogadishu

Four more days.

"I bring you tidings of great joy!"

Little Rock vs. Big Rock

GAY BAN MUST GO

Clinton Tells Military Chiefs

"Friendly fire."

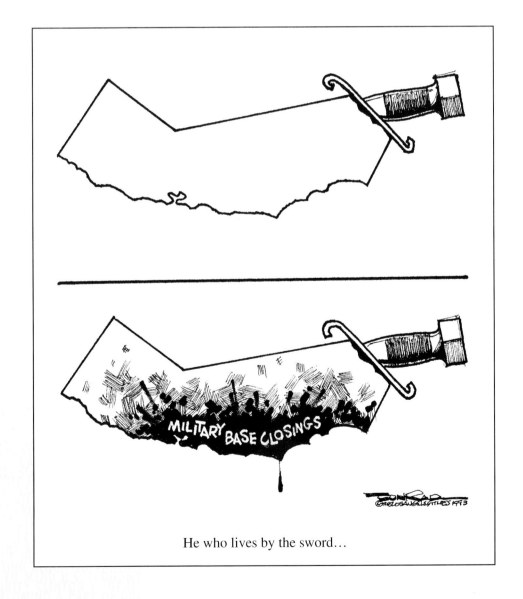

He who lives by the sword…

the Sixties *

Page 8: "Stand back everybody! He's got a bomb!!" (May 6, 1963); "Fifteen yards for pushing!" "Fifteen yards for holding!" (October 23, 1963) **Page 9:** 'Anybody got a match?' (July 5, 1963); '…The Great Buddha has answered our prayers!' (November 5, 1963) **Page 10:** "It looked back!" (Kennedy, Khurshchev, March 20, 1963); "Well, if their money is good enough for the Canadians, it's good enough for me!" (September 24, 1963); 'All those in favor of the test-ban treaty will signify…' (August 7, 1963) **Page 11:** "The time has come," the Walrus said, "to talk of many things: Of cloture votes, and civil rights, and Martin Luther Kings." (May 28, 1964); "Shall we be trotting home again?" But answer came there none—And this was scarcely odd, because they'd eaten every one. (Passage of the Civil Rights Bill of 1964, June 15, 1964) **Page 12:** 'Someone's been eating my porridge,' said the Daddy Bear. (May 24, 1963) **Page 13:** Only the Names Have Been Changed (August 17, 1964); '10…9…8…7…6…5…' (China as 'little girl with a daisy' from Johnson campaign ad, October 2, 1964) **Page 14:** A Letter from the Front (Selma, March 23, 1965); "I call on every law enforcement officer…"–President Johnson. (Alabama state national guard federalized to protect civil rights marchers from Selma to Montgomery, March 29, 1965) **Page 15:** "Take me to a leader!" (Watts, August 17, 1965); "You've mentioned unemployment, housing, education, police brutality, and despair…but, what was the reason for the riot?" (August 30, 1965) **Page 16:** "There's a lady out in Mason City, Iowa, he can't seem to convince!" (August 4, 1965); "First, Premier Ky, you must learn the principles of democracy" (May 22, 1966) **Page 17:** "Tenting tonight, Tenting tonight, Tenting on the Old School Ground." (Mississippi state police drive civil rights marchers from the grounds of a Canton school, June 27, 1966); "Excuse me…I thought that sort of thing was unconstitutional!" (May 19, 1966); Majority Whip (October 10, 1966) **Page 18:** Reagan for Governor Rehearsal – 8:00 AM – Sharp. (June 10, 1966); "Wha'd'ya mean…'He doesn't know the territory'…?" (October 29, 1967) **Page 19:** You are Now Entering Redwood National Park (June 27, 1968) **Page 20:** Flag Razing in Central Park (April 18, 1967); "Pick a number between 20,000 and 100,000…" (Westmoreland, McNamara, Johnson, July 17, 1967) **Page 21:** "Martin Luther who…?" April 7, 1967; Speaking of forcing North Vietnam to its knees… (May 8, 1967) **Page 22:** "Don't turn my dream into a nightmare…!" (The assassination of Martin Luther King, Jr., April 7, 1968); Reflecting Pool (People's March on Washington, led by Ralph Abernathy, May 26, 1968) **Page 23:** One and One-half Million Primary Votes for Kennedy (The assassination of Robert F. Kennedy, June 7, 1968) **Page 24:** "It became necessary to destroy the party to save it!" (Hubert Humphrey, August 30, 1968) **Page 25:** "…Fascist…!" (September 1, 1968) **Page 26:** Do Not Bend, Fold or Debate This Candidate (October 17, 1968) **Page 27:** "I've got to go now…I've been appointed Secretary of Defense and the Secret Service men are here!" (November 13, 1968); 'Ye shall find the babe wrapped in swaddling clothes, lying in a manger.' (December 25, 1968) **Page 28:** Manrise. (First lunar landing, July 21, 1969) **Page 29:** "If you don't mind, Senator I'd rather walk…" (Chappaquiddick, September 4, 1969); Troop Withdrawal (June 10, 1969); The Sound of Marching Effete (November 13, 1969)

the Seventies

Page 32: Poll reports more Americans disturbed over My Lai publicity than My Lai massacre itself. (January 7, 1970) **Page 33:** "Shut it down! Shut it down! Shut it down!" (May 8, 1970); "Son…!" "Dad…!" (May 13, 1970) **Page 34:** Blanket Party (May 20, 1970) **Page 35:** "HIT 'EM AGAIN—HIT 'EM AGAIN—HARDER—HARDER!" (November 4, 1970); "F.B.Me…Hoover speaking…" (April 16, 1971); There are cats and there are fat cats… (July 14, 1969) **Page 36:** Prison Reform (September 15, 1971) **Page 37:** "Oh, it's just kind of a hobby with me…!" (May 28, 1972) **Page 38:** "It only hurts when I laugh!" (May 6, 1971); Reagan Hood—He Takes From the Poor and Gives to the Rich! (December 18, 1972) **Page 39:** Commercial TV Fare (February 10, 1972); "…one nation, divisible, with liberty and justice for some." (March 21, 1972) **Page 40:** "Dear Mrs. Nixon and Julie: I appreciate your offer to give your lives…" (September 21, 1972) **Page 41:** 46,000 GI's, transfusion to Thieu. (September 5, 1971); The Light at the End of the Tunnel. (April 7, 1972) **Page 42:** "…Four more years? Four more years?…" (December 20, 1972) **Page 43:** "Let's overthrow the government!" "Which government?" (March 22, 1973); Chile (September 14, 1973) **Page 44:** "He says he's from the phone company…" (September 11, 1972); You know nothing about Watergate. Which group…? (June 8, 1973) **Page 45:** The Web (June 19, 1973) **Page 46:** His Own Worst Enemy (July 1, 1973) **Page 47:** "Oh, nothing much…what's new with you, John?" (July 12, 1973); "YOU'RE sick of hearing about Watergate!" (August 2, 1974) **Page 48:** "O that I were as great as my grief, or lesser than my name!" (July 22, 1973) **Page 49:** "Alas, poor Agnew, Mitchell, Stans, Ehrlichman…" (October 17, 1973); The King is Dead—Long Live the Presidency! (August 9, 1974) **Page 50:** Pardon of the pardon. (October 20, 1974) **Page 51:** Turning the Economy Around (January 24, 1975); "I pledge allegiance to the flag of the country that gives me the best deal…" (January 5, 1975) **Page 52:** Statue of Liberty with binoculars, microphone. (March 10, 1975); "And the first shall be last and the last first." (Hoover and King, November 30, 1975) **Page 53:** 'Our long national nightmare is over…' (April 29, 1975); 'Victory finds a hundred fathers—defeat is an orphan.' (May 11, 1975); The African Queen: Aid for Angola (Ford and Kissinger, January 29, 1976) **Page 54:** "I was maybe the last Vietnam casualty." (May 30, 1977); Nixon nailing himself to the cross. (May 22, 1977) **Page 55:** Souvenir stand at Casa Pacifica. (February 26, 1978) **Page 56:** Stoop Labor

* Dates listed refer to date of publication.

(January 30, 1976); "My name is Juan Garcia and I could use your help here in California!" (May 23,1976) **Page 57:** "Brother Brown is in conference…can I help you? (July 29, 1975); "It looks like Brother Brown has gone over the wall!" (March 20, 1977) **Page 58:** "…1980 on your dial…" (September 6, 1976); "No country has ever observed the terms of a treaty if it suited its national purposes to break that treaty." (September 13, 1977) **Page 59:** Senior Citizens' Apartments (July 9, 1974); The world as a starving child. (August 5, 1974) **Page 60:** 'Forgive them, Father, for they know not what they do…' (July 2, 1976) **Page 61:** The Butcher's Thumb (July 6, 1976) **Page 62:** "There's no waste problem…we just dig a new hole!" (January 26, 1976); I Love (Canal) New York. (May 25, 1980); Noah's animals climbing out of the smog. (August 7, 1970) **Page 63:** Noah's animals climbing out of an oily sea. (January 31, 1977) **Page 64:** "You wanta take away our gusto…?" (January 9, 1978); The California Syndrome (May 21, 1979) **Page 65:** Hara-Cari (July 9, 1980) **Page 66:** Jimmy Carter: "I have lusted…" (September 23, 1976) **Page 67:** "I am under the magic spell of the wicked Congressional witch. Kiss me and I become the President of the United States!" (June 27, 1978) **Page 68:** Vatican prohibits ordination of women as priests because Christ's representatives must have a 'natural resemblance' to him. (February 1, 1977); "Joan, you still have time to recant!" (November 30, 1977) **Page 69:** "Sexism, hell! We did the same thing to Earl Warren!" (October 8, 1978) **Page 70:** "Gimme a white! Gimme a male!…" (September 28, 1977) **Page 71:** "Dere Sirs—" (October 30, 1977); Black Teen-agers 40% Unemployed. (December 2, 1977) **Page 72:** Speaking of child pornography… (November 1, 1977) **Page 73:** …and for those who made the 1977 Nobel Peace Prize necessary…(Awarded to Amnesty International, October 12, 1977); Terrorist holds airliner hostage. (October 19, 1977) **Page 74:** Latter-Day Israelites Wandering 40 Years in the Wilderness (October 21, 1973); A future Horowitz, a future Einstein, a future Salk… (March 20, 1978); Menachem Begin welcomes Anwar Sadat at the inn. (November 16, 1977) **Page 75:** Carter as Sisyphus. (September 6, 1978); The Eighth Wonder of the World (September 21, 1978) **Page 76:** The Shah of Iran on Carter's shoulders on crumbling pedestal: "Human Rights" (December 13, 1978) **Page 77:** The Oilatollah Khompanies (February 25, 1979); "…Decontrol!…Decontrol!…Decontrol!…" (March 22, 1979); Khomeini giving the world the finger. (November 30, 1979) **Page 78:** "P.S. Please send us 50 Absentee ballots—" (April 10, 1980); "Now that the issues have become more manageable…" (May 2, 1980); "Do I hear $225,000…?" (Billy Carter registers as agent of Libya, July 25, 1980) **Page 79:** "Entrapment!" (Abscam investigation of congressmen, February 6, 1980); Camelot with Chappaquiddick bridge. (October 21, 1979) **Page 80:** Lord of the Flies (Medflies, July 14, 1981) **Page 81:** "You people are nothing but functional illiterates anyway!" (September 18, 1978); Friendly Fire (Eulia Love police shooting, April 29, 1979)

the Eighties

Page 84: Chief Daryl F. Gates presents LOS ANGELES NOW. (L.A.P.D. at May Day demonstration, May 5, 1980) **Page 85:** "I pick my arrows out of thin air." (April 13, 1980) **Page 86:** "You look for a certain compatibility, a broad compatibility, with your own philosophy in looking for judges." (October 8, 1980) **Page 87:** U.S. declares victory in war on poverty, and pulls out. (November 24, 1980); "You don't look truly needy to me…Needy, perhaps, but not truly needy!" (February 25, 1981) **Page 88:** "What's so terrible about 'black lung'…?" (March 11, 1981); Living proof that guns don't necessarily kill people…! (May 26, 1981); Reflections on Mrs. Reagan's new White House china. (September 15, 1981) **Page 89:** Trickle-down Theory (November 16, 1981); The first notch. (Air traffic controllers fired, August 10, 1981) **Page 90:** The Buck Stops in Alabama, Alaska, Arisona, Arkansas… (January 31, 1982) **Page 91:** "Dear Gov. Deukmejian: Who paid for *your* education?" (June 3, 1983); "Gov. Deukmejian, you are charged with vetoing the strip-and-search bill…Please bend over…" (October 5, 1983); Affixing blame for our economic problems. (September 30, 1982) **Page 92:** *Solidarnsc* (Martial law continues in Poland, January 18, 1982) **Page 93:** The PLO, Begin with the world as soccer ball. (July 15, 1982) **Page 94:** "I exist…therefore…I am…or else!" (July 23, 1982); Massacre at Sabra and Shatila refugee camps. (September 20, 1982) **Page 95:** El Salvador. (The Domino Theory, February 7, 1982); In memory of the 30,000 Argentine "disappeared ones" the Pope didn't see. (June 13, 1982) **Page 96:** "Then it's agreed…You'll take care of the poor and I'll take care of the rich!" (June 10, 1982) **Page 97:** "Well, tell him to turn up his hearing aid!" (Lebanon, September 12, 1983); The War Powers Actor (September 29, 1983) **Page 98:** "Buy a pentagon nut for only $260 billion…and get this FREE!!" (November 17, 1983); Christmas tree made of missiles, submarines, warplanes, tanks… (December 20, 1983) **Page 99:** The Big Dipper (May 9, 1985); F-1 Fighter anatomized. (July 6, 1981) **Page 100:** Administration's civil-defense plan for nuclear war. (January 21, 1982); "We'll bury you!" (March 13, 1984) **Page 101:** "I'm willing to discuss the arms race whenever those Russian devils are!" (June 18, 1984) **Page 102:** "NOTICE – This bombshelter closed because of underground seepage of water contaminated by dioxins." (April 22, 1983) **Page 103:** "I'm nobody's puppet!" (Anne Burford, March 4, 1983); Watt-Man (March 26, 1982) **Page 104:** "Now, about the rules…" (May 24, 1984) **Page 105:** The Tell-Tale Hart (March 6, 1984); "WE ARE somebody…!" (April 6, 1984) **Page 106:** "Let's face it, Fritz—You're no Harry Truman, and I'm no Lauren Bacall!" (Geraldine Ferraro, November 5, 1984); "Religion and politics are necessarily related." (September 5, 1984) **Page 107:** "You're on your own, kid, once you're born!" (February 3, 1984) **Page 108:** The Man in the Teflon-Coated Suit (May 6, 1984) **Page 109:** "My candle burns at both ends…" (April 20, 1984); Vast worldwide misinformation machine. (May 31, 1984) **Page 110:** People want to believe. (October 21, 1984); "I've never worn makeup." (October 12, 1984) **Page 111:** "Four more years!" (November 7, 1984) **Page 112:** "Let's walk Gramm, Rudman and Hollings to get to Reagan!" (October 22, 1985); "Have I got a deal for you!" (April 12, 1984) **Page 113:** The difference between 'overt' and 'covert' CIA military actions. (William Casey, May 16, 1983); C.I.A. Assassination Manual (October 22, 1984) **Page 114:** "Nicaraguan *contras*…the moral equal of our Founding Fathers." (March 8, 1985) **Page 115:** "Don't none of you sanctuary people move!" (November 15, 1985) **Page 116:** Reagan in bathtub with warships, aircraft carriers, rubber duckie. (Show of force off coast of Libya, March 27, 1986); "We have done what we had to do. If necessary, we will do it again." (Reagan as Kadafi: U.S. bombs Libya, April 16, 1986); **Page 117:** Mother Russia (Afghanistan, April 29, 1984) **Page 118:** Ask not for whom the reactor tolls; it tolls for thee. (Chernobyl, May 6, 1986) **Page 119:** Three-minute egg. (June 16, 1986) **Page 120:** …and touched the face of God. (Challenger spacecraft disaster, January 31, 1986) **Page 121:** O-ring (June 11, 1986) **Page 122:** Photo opportunity. (August 8, 1986); The knock on the bedroom door. (Supreme Court upholds Georgia sodomy law, July 2, 1986) **Page 123:** "Justice Rehnquist, will you be wearing your hooded white or your black robe today?" (September 11, 1986); "And I resent the left-wing attempts to politicize my Supreme Court appointments!" (November 13, 1987) **Page 124:** The poor don't know where to go to get food. (May 26, 1986) **Page 125:** Home for Christmas. (December 25, 1986) **Page 126:** "It's a privilege to shake the hand of a freedom fighter!" (June 22, 1986) **Page 127:** Reagan Administration's moral compass. (December 15, 1986); The naked truth. (February 17, 1987) **Page 128:** Ollie's World (July 12, 1987); Oliver North swearing to tell the whole truth. (February 26, 1987) **Page 129:** "We needed a ship." (July 19, 1987); CIA gives *contras* detailed profiles of civilian targets. (March 23, 1987) **Page 130:** You *can* take it with you! (William Casey, May 10, 1987); "Thank you for not smoking." (August 6, 1987) **Page 131:** Conscience of a conservative. (February 19, 1988); Reagan operated from computer behind screen. (March 3, 1988) **Page 132:** "Dear Diary—Again today, nobody told me anything about selling arms to Iran…" (February 2, 1990) **Page 133:** "We don't do junk bonds anymore…just bail bonds!" (November 20, 1986); The leveraged buyout (how it really works). (April 17, 1988) **Page 134:** Deregulation (November 23, 1987); The American Banking Association's drive-thru window. (April 25, 1983) **Page 135:** Hands Across America (May 28, 1986); "Can't you see that we're busy with this humanitarian liver transplant?" (August 15, 1983) **Page 136:** The President faces the AIDS question. (June 12, 1987); Speaking of the need for condoms… (February 22, 1987) **Page 137:** Reagan 'shooting up' with military rifle. (Troops to Honduras for maneuvers, March 18, 1988) **Page 138:** Administration war against drugs in Bolivia…and in the U.S.A. (July 20, 1986) **Page 139:** The Sorcerer's Apprentice (May 12, 1988) **Page 140:** Another gang terrorizing U.S. cities. (April 20, 1988) **Page 141:** Morning in America (March 27, 1988); The Mitsubishi Rockettes (November 2, 1989); Drawing up the will. (March 14, 1988) **Page 142:** "Ta da!" (June 2, 1988); Perestroika (June 6, 1988); Abraham and Isaac (February 7, 1988) **Page 143:** The greenhouse effect. (August 2, 1988); Nuclear weapons plant. (December 18, 1988); Acid rain. (April 10, 1987) **Page 144:** Evangelical Testimonial Dinner (March 27, 1987) **Page 145:** Popemobile. (September 14, 1987); Jesse Jackson's grandmother's quilt. (Keynote speech at Democratic Convention, July 21, 1988) **Page 146:** Bush and Quayle with balloons going up. (October 23, 1988) **Page 147:** No Heart, No Brains, No Courage (November 1, 1988) **Page 148:** Passing the torch. (July 10, 1988); "Horseshoes, Lee—just horseshoes!" (June 13, 1989) **Page 149:** "Dear Mr. President: Too bad about William Lucas…" (August 4, 1989) **Page 150:** Monument to the First Amendment (June 23, 1989) **Page 151:** "The face on the barroom floor." (July 3, 1989) **Page 152:** State Government Property – U.S. Supreme Court (July 12, 1989); "Their daddy, George Deukmejian, doesn't believe in family planning." (July 26, 1989); Molested by her father, raped by a stranger, abandoned by her President. (October 20, 1989) **Page 153:** Prospective jurors for the North trial who have no knowledge of the Iran-Contra affair. (Reagan, Meese, Bush, Deaver, Abrams, MacFarlane, Baker, Nancy…, February 2, 1989); White collar: Probation, Blue collar: Jail Term (Oliver North verdict, July 10, 1989) **Page 154:** Fudget of the United States Government (January 12, 1989); "Piker!" (July 19, 1989) **Page 155:** The ex-Presidents at work. (October 31, 1989) **Page 156:** "Just say dough!" (November 7, 1989) **Page 157:** "We spent your children's and your grandchildren's inheritance." (May 1, 1990); "It's Frankie…just say no." (April 10, 1991) **Page 158:** El Salvador (Made in U.S.A., November 17, 1989); El Salvador (Six Jesuit priests and two members of their household killed, December 15, 1989) **Page 159:** DIVIDE, or DIE (October 2, 1989) **Page 160:** E. Germany, Poland, Hungary, Czechoslovakia…flowers from snow. (December 3, 1989) **Page 161:** Humpty Dumpty sat on a wall… (November 24, 1989); The Berlin Wall broken. (December 25, 1989)

the Nineties

Page 164: The Post-Stalin Era/The Post-Reagan Era (May 10, 1990) **Page 165:** One man, 28 million votes. (Nelson Mandela, February 18, 1990); World War II ain't over 'til the fat lady sings! (July 20, 1990) **Page 166:** U.S.S. Kinder, U.S.S. Gentler (January 12, 1990) **Page 167:** LET THEM EAT BROCCOLI! (March 29, 1990); The hummingbird consumes twice its own body weight daily. (April 5, 1990) **Page 168:** If you thought Dukakis looked silly in that tank… (June 4, 1990) **Page 169:** "Health Care? What do you think I'm made of…MONEY?" (June 3, 1990) **Page 170:** Charles Keating's Washington holdings. (March 11, 1990) **Page 171:** 2 Live Crew. (June 20, 1990) **Page 172:** A jury to decide obscenity laws. (October 4, 1990) **Page 173:** "Dad, they're calling up the reserves!" (August 23, 1990); Bush loaded for battle, pants down: Recession. (August 29, 1990) **Page 174:** "Keep going! The line Bush drew in the sand is here someplace!" (October 15, 1990); Reaganstein's Saddam (November 5, 1990) **Page 175:** Cormorant, olive branch soaked in oil. (Persian Gulf, January 29, 1991); "Wolfe was right. You can't go home again." (Exxon Valdez, April 17, 1989); Bush's thousand points of light. (January 31, 1991) **Page 176:** Saddam Hussein sat on a wall, Saddam Hussein refuses to fall… (February 21, 1991) **Page 177:** Line in the sand. (February 26, 1991) **Page 178:** Joe Rosenthal's photo of the flag-raising on Iwo Jima if journalists had been pooled in World War II. (Panama invasion, January 17, 1990); CNN's Peter Arnett reporting from Baghdad/U.S. media reporting from Pentagon briefing. (February 24, 1991) **Page 179:** The Republican Guard (March 8, 1991) **Page 180:** "I have drawn a line in the blood." (April 5, 1991); The homecoming parade. (May 19, 1991) **Page 181:** Dances with Wolves. (March 21, 1991) **Page 182:** Gorbachev, crumbling U.S.S.R. birthmark. (August 28, 1991); Mother Russia. (Pregnant Liberty, July 21, 1991) **Page 183:** Will Work for Food – Yeltsin (March 22, 1992) **Page 184:** The Education President…The Transportation President (September 1, 1991); "We come to bury Cranston, not to praise him…." (November 22, 1991) **Page 185:** Death Row (Supreme Court limits death penalty appeals, April 19, 1991); Justice Thurgood Marshall sat here. (September 2, 1991); "Seen any good porno movies lately?" (October 17, 1991) **Page 186:** "Would you buy a NEW car from this man?" (January 7, 1992); Bush seeks to kill luxury tax on yachts. (January 29, 1992) **Page 187:** History of California redwoods. (June 25, 1990); "Well, there goes the neighborhood!" (May 18, 1992) **Page 188:** "You have the right to remain sick…" (February 7, 1992) **Page 189:** Daryl Gates (July 10, 1991); One picture is worth zero. (April 30, 1992); The Melted Pot (May 15, 1992) **Page 190:** You Build a Party, They'll Come! (July 17, 1991); The Final Four (March 25, 1992) **Page 191:** Clinton on sax, Bush on trumpet, Perot on triangle. (June 10, 1992); When the going gets tough, the tough get going. (July 17, 1992) **Page 192:** Family Values. (June 25, 1992); "Family Values." (July 19, 1992) **Page 193:** "What do you wanta' be if you grow up?" (September 21, 1992) **Page 194:** "We have a totally clear conscience." (June 16, 1992) **Page 195:** Devolution of Man to grave: AIDS. (July 31, 1992); Navy fighter with women downed. (Tailhook sexual harassment case, July 5, 1992) **Page 196:** What to do about Iraqgate. (April 29, 1992); …And now for the *real* trick! (October 1, 1991) **Page 197:** The Liar's Club (September 23, 1992); The Reagan Bush (March 28, 1993) **Page 198:** Pardons happen. (Bush pardons Weinberger, other Iran-Contra figures, December 29, 1992); The Nine Lives of Richard Nixon (December 14, 1992) **Page 199:** Pillory Clinton (August 20, 1992); "Shoot, if you must, this old gray head…" (September 9, 1992); Bush at campaign whistlestop, train pulls off without him. (October 22, 1992) **Page 200:** Dish Raising at Mogadishu (December 10, 1992); Four more days. (January 17, 1993) **Page 201:** "I bring you tidings of great joy!" (December 25, 1992); Little Rock vs. Big Rock (December 18, 1992) **Page 202:** Perot: "I told you so!" (February 17, 1993); General thumbs nose at Clinton, order lifting ban on gays. (January 28, 1993) **Page 203:** "Friendly fire." (February 7, 1993); He who lives by the sword… (March 10, 1993)